Daddy – I hope you [will get lots]
of enjoyment reading this – maybe it
will give you some ideas!

Happy Birthday love Fan.
x
'08

THE SHED
BOOK

GORDON THORBURN AND GARETH JONES

THE SHED BOOK

CONTENTS

6

SHEDS AND SHEDDISTS

Let us begin in the Dark Ages and in a shady place, because the modern English word "shed" comes from the Anglo-Saxon for shade, *scead*, pronounced "shay-ud", which is how they still say it in certain northern districts of England.

Scead, of course, means partial darkness or comparative obscurity. These are fundamental concepts in understanding what made a Sheddist originally. He was a kind of wise man, a hermit, an oracle. He was partially dark and comparatively obscure but ordinary folk knew he was different, in a very special way.

Over the years, the old concept of shed – hermit's retreat – developed extra shades of meaning. The hermit assembled things around him, some with magical significance. He collected strange objects, the importance of which others could not understand, and worked on them with his hands. His shed became his intellectual pantry, his workshop, his spiritual home.

SHEDDISM NOW

Some of the Sheddists in this book have chosen to interpret this ancient tradition to the letter and stay in their sheds all day, every day, making a living at it. There are potters who pot, inventors who invent, a chap who sings 'Crystal Chandeliers' all the time, a fellow who carves ducks and swans, and a poltergeist hunter.

For others, the shed itself is the thing and the way it's kitted out. There's the British Railways guard's van restored to glory, and the fisherman's grotto, and the state-of-the-art recording studio.

Some men are obsessed by the unusual items they put in their sheds. Some have made their sheds their social hub, inviting the like-minded inside to share that certain whatever-it-is. Some have not the slightest idea and don't care a jot or tittle. For many, though, it's the escape thing. They admit it. A hobby might be the raison d'être on the surface but, as they say on "The X Files", the truth is in there.

HOW DID IT EVOLVE?

Scientists may postulate that Sheddism, like ginger hair and sticky-out ears, is genetic. This book contains evidence for such a proposal, for example, the man whose uncle made the first wireless set in their street. Contrarily, there is also evidence for the Big Bang theory as with the man who, unaware of the life-shaping importance of his action, picked up a brick on the beach.

Most Sheddists and Sheddism experts do, however, agree on a quite different premise, which is to do with sex. In these days of political correctness, such an issue is difficult and dangerous to face but it is clear that the ladies, bless them, are simply not in the shed. Is this because they lack the Shedding instinct, or is it something more sinister?

Are blokes Sheddists only by consent? Perhaps the ladies allow us to construct our hideaways so we can escape from the house and get away from her indoors.

MIRROR, MIRROR, ON THE SHED WALL

We have to ask each Sheddist to examine the following scenes. Is there anything here, anything at all, which you recognise and which therefore might help us with our inquiries into the nature of Sheddism?

The women do it by hints. Sometimes the hint is no more than the flicker of a seductive eyelash, a slight pursing of the lips, or that special little tickly thing she does with her index finger on the end of your nose.

Sometimes it's a few words, spoken subtly and without any kind of imperative. These words might be along the lines of "How are you getting on with your glider/milk bottles/steam engine/working model of Space Station Mir made entirely out of grass clippings?"

Or, she might say "How do you expect me to get on with my womanly, feminine tasks with a great fat useless idle ugly wart like you under my feet the whole time?"

If we chaps are being dismissed to our sheds, why is that? Why have they not moved in beside us? They play our Rugby League, spot our train numbers, understand the offside and LBW laws – what's going on?

SHEDDISM -V- MODERNISM

Things accumulate in sheds, originally wanted then forgotten and much later resurrected as momentous mementoes. Old magazines like *Picture Post* for instance. A favourite of mine had an advert for a car showing a standard American family admiringly boarding a huge and ugly late 1950s car, under the headline "We're not the richest folks in town. We just look it."

Sheddists are not outraged by this impossibly naïve drivel. Sheddists smile at the idea of everyone in town writing you begging letters and asking you to be mayor, just because you have seated yourself in a colourful carriage of bent tin resembling a shark-shaped jukebox.

Signs hung on shed walls say things like *Guinness is good for you*, *Craven 'A' cigarettes will not harm your throat* and *Bovril prevents that sinking feeling*, invalid scientifically but so what? The public once was given credit for common sense. They got the message without believing the advertisement. Nowadays, while the rest of the world has gone barking mad, Sheddists retain that traditional sense of what is right and good.

SHEDDISM AND QUIET ENJOYMENT

As a very small boy, your correspondent lived in a village in north Yorkshire where father was the village policeman. The house had no mains water but it did have a shed, up the field.

Regular use was made of this shed which was fitted with a small, pale wooden roller hanging on a piece of rusty wire and a polished wooden seat with a large hole in it. A man came to empty the shed every once in a while.

In that golden age, although sound and music were not yet the norm of the world, a shed was still a welcome refuge. Today, those who seek peace and quiet might be regarded as slightly odd by those norms who revel in constantly available music plugged into their ears, broadcast in their cars, at work and, crime of crimes, in the pub, but that's what sheds are all about. Here's to tranquillity.

Gordon Thorburn

"CORKSCREW STARBOARD – GO!"

...as the WW2 gunners used to order their bomber pilots when they were attacked by a fighter. One day, Lyndon will make his shed-top gun turret rotate so he can take evasive action while shooting imaginary Junkers 88s. Meanwhile, he's busy with his seven-piece visual orchestra, the Busk-O-Matic. His players (see picture: Lyndon is the one in the middle) blow smoke rings, bubbles and showers of sparks.

Lyndon's day job is managing and flying aerial surveys, like the one precisely mapping new routes for London's tube. When he returns to his shed it's his mind which is flying, producing a string of world firsts: the propeller-powered wickerwork car, the amphibious bathchair, the amphibious tricycle and the world's first conversion of a 1922 Citroën to wickerwork (yes, he likes wickerwork).

If anyone has a pair of Browning .303 machine guns for the turret, contact: www.lyndonsmachines.co.uk.

"It's crackers but is it art?"

SHOP AT SHEDCO

Members of the Golders Green Allotment and Horticultural Society can fulfil all their earthy needs in the Gardeners' Bazaar, whose honorary proprietor is John, aged 84. Managing the enterprise, catering for 196 allotments, is second nature to someone who used to manage a large bakery.

Golders Green's north London oasis is a long way from Gold Beach, Normandy, on D-Day, where John was with the 8th Army Royal Engineers, but his army training is still useful. Now he has the mowers, rotavators and strimmers to maintain, bought with shop profits and hired out to members.

John's three-shed terrace, at the posh end of the shed spectrum, has stucco walls, a tiled roof and mod cons. The shop and storage are full of what every gardener wants – seeds, compost, canes, cloches, green string – and the office has what every horticultural provisioning executive deserves: a microwave and a kettle.

"We had 5 plots in 1913 – before my time of course."

HANDY ON THE ETHIOPIAN BANJO

Jim was an engineer making street lights. Illness forced him to retire so he turned himself into a highly skilled and remarkably expressive woodcarver.

Finding the wood at a decent price is difficult. He likes lime best – it must be very well seasoned – but he also works in oak. See the two old boys sitting on a bench? The one with the stick is Jim's late father-in-law, and the full-size stick is the duck's head by Jim's left hand, with a hazel shaft, a lime head, a mahogany beak, and a home-made nut and bolt to fix it together.

There is no design to start with. He looks at the wood and waits for an idea to come out of it, like the great hall with rooms off, the corral or the charioteer. Then he just sits in his chair in his shed, carving away or, for a change, renovating his friend's Ethiopian banjo. Young Albert's stick with the horse's head handle might have been the finest that Woolworth's could sell, but Jim sells nothing. To carve is the thing.

"I started when I heard 'Albert and the Lion'."

THE GARDENER'S ARMS

There'll be an analytical chemist somewhere who can prove that the atomic composition of a supermarket leek, sprout or runner bean is identical to that of your own allotment leek, sprout or runner bean. Scientists? They should stick to inventing the voice-activated doorknob.

True anti-scientists Dink, Robbo and Prem (reading from the left), are seen here meeting in the lounge bar of The Gardener's Arms for an organic discussion on the relative merits of Amsterdam Forcing and Chantenay Red Cored as general-purpose carrots in a dampish climate. As usual, the conversation has broadened into even more vital issues such as global warming, the price of hand-rolling tobacco and whether the Old Foxwhelp cider-apple tree needs supplementing, perhaps with a Strawberry Norman.

Provided the fuel for the stove lasts out and the homemade refreshments likewise, conviviality could persist into the late afternoon, making gardening completely unnecessary for another day.

"Stringless, with smooth, fleshy pods."

ORDOVICIAN IS THE WORD

While the first backbones were evolving into something approaching a fish, Martin's raw material was being formed. Called brick shale, this grey clay is Ordovician, 450 million years old, and is so rough it will take your skin off if you throw it on a wheel.

Ordinary clay, made more recently by glacial grinding, cannot give Martin the same feelings, nor can it offer the same challenges to his clients when, after admiring the lovely red it has become in firing, they try to lift the work they've commissioned. Large clay sculptures are normally hollow. Martin's brick shale sculptures are solid, limited in size only by the capacity of the kiln.

For smaller work, he still won't allow convention into his converted coalhouse. He likes Raku, the Japanese method of taking the item out of the kiln red hot and plunging it into sawdust. He gets more brightly coloured glazes that way.

22

"A Winged Victory for your garden?"

THE WORST LPs IN THE WORLD

Plastics company manager John is definitely in the escaping category of sheddists, keen to get away from the TV and the phone. He built the shed himself entirely out of old pallets with insulated double walls, extension and porch – but to his wife's orders. John uses the shed himself – but has to listen to his wife's choice of music.

Because of her 1950s fixation, this means John is an expert on Alma Cogan, Anne Shelton, Ronnie Hilton and so on, and he cordially hates them all. 'Songs that Won the War' is probably his least favourite, making him dive for the fitted refrigerator where the beer is kept. Wine and spirits are in the tasteful kitchen cupboard to his left. Friends come for meals in the winter, heated by John's stove which he brought back from France on a rugby bus. They reminisce about wooden tennis racquets, Bakelite telephones, 'Two-Way Family Favourites' and 'Music While You Work'. They should probably get out more.

"Homely cozy junk, really."

SHED IN THE PARK

Richard was a management accountant and university teacher but it's woodwork which satisfies his soul. After teaching himself the range of techniques, he's now happily making window frames, kitchen units, furniture, anything.

His house is called the Shippon – an old English word for cowshed – but his woodworking shed is his masterwork. Were it not in a National Park it would by now be a bijou residence. It had been used as a garage and Richard had to go through the planning hoops to be allowed to restore it back to a shed.

His best find was the wall which had been knocked down to make the garage doors. That was under the concrete floor. Richard dressed the stone and, with some lintels from a reclamation yard, his own windows and doors and stone flags in front, it's beginning to look rather upmarket, really. Still, nothing's too good for the sheddist classes.

"The house is the cowshed. The shed is no house."

27

ONE PUNCH BEYOND

Stephen's expanding paranormal activities have forced a move out of the house and into the garden shed. He's an expert on UFOs (mostly experimental aircraft, he believes) and parapsychology – the study of extrasensory perception. His growing reputation brings him work from the most unlikely quarters.

A council tenant complained about water in the house appearing from nowhere. Water is a regular feature of poltergeist infestation, which is usually connected with stress in those being infested. Stephen managed to collect some of this water. Laboratory tests showed it to have 30 times the normal reading for conductivity units. It was, literally, electrified.

On another poltergeist job, in front of two witnesses, Stephen received a mighty blow in his back which sent him flying, "like a punch combined with an electric shock. It's OK investigating but it's a bit much when the investigator becomes the victim."

"There's a rational explanation, usually."

IF IT CAN BE FIXED, IT WILL BE

Sheet steel is expensive. People throw washing machines on tips. Therefore, mend your Renault 4 rustbucket with rectangles of washing machine. This is a philosophy which Robin applies in his garage and which he takes with him into his shed.

His wife seems to be the main source of supply for his shed work. While Robin collects every kind of screw, nut, bit and piece in the world by dismantling every thrown-out food mixer or lawnmower that comes his way, his beloved brings home things she finds in skips, charity shops and car-boot sales. She knows that he will have the ability and the wherewithal to fix whatever, and she likes to keep him busy.

From rebuilding an exercise bike to mending jewellery to fixing a leather binding to making a buffing machine for antique brass, Robin is the man who can. One of his uncles built the first wireless set in his street. It's in the blood, that sort of thing.

30

"I'd quite like to read a book, really."

"I SLEPT WITH HARRY SECOMBE...

...in the same tent, when we were in the Army. We were part of the excitingly named Central Pool of Artists, along with Ken Platt, Norman Vaughan and others. I was a magician. Harry was a singer, gradually turning himself into a comedian."

Ralph at 78 and a member of the Magic Circle for 55 years, doesn't perform his magic professionally any more. He prefers to pass on his secrets to aspiring youngsters, fellows of the ancient Manchester Order of the Magi.

From magic to origami to plastic moulds for decorations may seem a curious route but it's all arts and crafts and that is Ralph's forte. He supplies play schemes, youth clubs and community projects with his moulds, produced on a vacuum-forming press in his shed, from originals he's made himself, or found. The moulds are virtually indestructible – a bit like Ralph.

"My act used to be the drunk with the lamp-post."

A PROFUSELY DRILLED SKIRT

The pile of bits on the floor of Hicky's shed included the front axle, the 4.3 litre 4-cylinder engine, the gear box and a few other useful items. The rear axle and the chassis were elsewhere, somewhere, and there was no bodywork at all, or wheels, but these were minor inconveniences compared to the exciting possibility of rebuilding the oldest competition Sunbeam in the world (see picture).

Hicky says this is the works hill-climb car, one of only three 1911 Sunbeam 16/20s left. He made the aluminium body, following photographs and a contemporary description which gave it a profusely drilled skirt. He made the wicker seats, too. Hicky's friends say they can't tell where his shed stops and his house begins, which may be something to do with the various states of repair of his 1903 Peugeot, 1909 Cadillac, 1913 Star, 1916 5.7 V8 Cadillac, 1917 Dodge, 1928 hill-climb special Riley/Rover and other evidence, if it were needed, of his life-long fascination. And, at intervals, he is still heard to murmur 'Poop-poop!'

"I'm a sporting person, not a polishing person."

WHAT'S THE DIFFERENCE BETWEEN A DUCK?

One leg is both the same, of course, which rather sums up Guy's route through life. He designed a lady's head on a stick for a level-crossing sign, to make people notice it more. Another dark, driftwood head was stolen by children who left it propped up against a front door and almost frightened a poor old lady pensioner to death.

Such matters seem inevitable to Guy, who discovered his gift for wood-art while minding the ducks in Regent's Park. He started with a small axe, making decoy-type ducks, and people wanted to buy them, so it was but a short step to mute swans (stylised, see picture), West End galleries, magazine articles and TV.

He's withdrawn a little now, to the gentler lights of small local galleries, but he still has the same approach. He likes estuary driftwood but he doesn't look for shapes inside it. He wants a big block that he can draw and cut out with a bandsaw. How do you make a duck? Well, you get a piece of wood and you...

"...chop everything off that don't look like a duck."

150 LIGHTS AND 2000 CRYSTALS, OR SMALLER

When Joseph arrived in the UK from Iraq he didn't know what an antique was and he'd never seen a chandelier. A job in an antique shop led to chandeliers in his bedroom and, soon, to a shed. He had to build it. There's a limit to how many chandeliers you can get in a bedroom.

There's a limit in the shed, too, but Joseph doesn't want to step beyond it for the moment. He's happy going to antique fairs in Belgium and France, buying the chandeliers of old, restoring them and selling them to a never-ending line of customers who prefer to deal with him rather than a big company.

In the line recently was a Saudi sheikh who wanted his 1860 French Empire £150,000 chandelier done up and hung. It measured twelve metres by eight, which is three times bigger than Joseph's shed. Otherwise, Joseph's customers are everyday town and country folk who just happen to fancy some *fin de siècle* twinkling grandeur in the sitting room, at a modest price.

"My style, not just any old chandelier."

THE SECRET LIFE OF A TAXMAN

Out of his shed, he is exactly like an ordinary chap. He goes to the office (Inland Revenue), works, comes home, leaves stuff lying about the house and gets moaned at by his wife for making the place untidy. Then, he goes to his shed and is transformed. Terry, in the cramped confines of his workshop, becomes Super Orderly Recycling Man.

Every tool has its hand-carved peg so, when finished with, it can hang at perfect right angles to its neighbour. Every project, unless *in extremis*, is made with left-over this and that. A left-over door became some new flooring in the house, a left-over bedside cabinet became a wall-mounted display case, bits of left-over timber became a model aeroplane and a folding table with model race track attached. The chimney breast in the dining room, left over after the central heating was installed, became a built-in Welsh dresser. Left over from his youth is a Sun calendar for 1984. It's on his shed wall, permanently open at Linda Lusardi.

40

"We're awash with CDs, but I've wood left over."

SELL, OR OPEN A MUSEUM?

John started small with steam before moving into combustion engines. His first was a Lister D petrol/paraffin which, in the old days, drove the vacuum pump which milked the cows in just about every milking parlour in the country. Lister made 600,000 of these static engines, used to power everything imaginable, and taking his to a rally was enough to set John in search of bigger, rarer and increasingly challenging machines.

His biggest was a 16HP Crossley Horizontal, 35cwt, which drove the cast-iron rollers in a mortar pan, crushing ashes and lime into powder. His rarest was a Boulton and Paul from 1924. John also built all four of his sheds but, after falling off the roof of one, breaking his back and his neck, he will not be building any more. His injury also means he can't cart the really big engines around to exhibit, so some of the collection, if it's to be seen, must be sold. The one in the picture he classes as medium – a 5HP Petter, originally used to drive a concrete mixer. But what's that thing in the corner?

"It's a searchlight off a fire engine."

BRICK TRIGGERS CLICK

Scientists believe that dozens of behavioural traits lie latent within everyone, waiting for that unexpected sight or sound to flick the switch. For many of us, the stimulus to brick collecting never operates. For Angus it did, in 1989. He can tell you when, and where – walking along a beach – he first picked up a brick, but he cannot tell you why.

Once started, he couldn't stop. He didn't care about the small gangs of children running after him, hoping he was looking for money. Having scoured his own locale pretty well, Angus now sets off in his car to beaches, demolition sites, old collieries and fly tips where he may find a duplicate, to be kept outside the shed for swapping with other collectors (yes, there are several), or a specimen he's never seen or heard of before. His interest is not in every Tom, Dick and Harry of a brick. Only those with makers' names and marks are deemed suitable for recording by sketch and note in his catalogues. He likes to be able to classify them by place of origin and to list them by county.

"But I'm quite happy just to have them."

TALK, WALK AND CHARGE AT THE SAME TIME

Trevor was no great scholar but he could produce the most astounding essays with his Meccano set. That's the way his mind works, translating dreams into practical reality by way of an engineer's hands and ten thousand washing machine components. The shed provides the space and wherewithal to put the invention, the idea he couldn't mention in case they laughed, which became that bizarre contraption spread all over the bench, into a box which can then be called a product.

It was in his shed that the famous clockwork radio was invented. More recently it's been the electric shoe, which puts a small recharge into your mobile phone battery every time you put one foot in front of another. Also rechargeable is the device which fits in your ear and teaches you basic English for an hour, 'you' being – for starters anyway – 140 million Chinese. A few words of English can transform a life in such a country. Trevor's ideas are like that. For more inspiration, attend the inventors' forum on www.thetbf.org.uk

"I give myself enough room to be original."

THE ART OF THE UNIVERSE

Fifteen years ago, you would have needed a million dollar telescope, a massive building and a mainframe computer to do what Alan does. Now, for rather less than the cost of small car, he has the technology and the purpose-built observatory, artfully designed to look exactly like a garden shed so it fits in with the flowers that surround it.

His reflecting telescope is moved about the sky by software Alan has written himself. We can see only two galaxies with the naked eye: our own Milky Way and Andromeda, a mere two million light years away. Alan's looking three or four hundred million light years away, at the thousands of galaxies which exist up to that distance. There are billions more but, for the moment, you still need the million dollar job to see them. His built-in camera system takes digital images of his galaxies and these pictures are his real passion. Not for him the endless search for a new comet. He prefers the beauty of the known but, until recently, invisible universe. See his pictures on www.ajefferis.freeserve.co.uk

"10" Schmidt-Cassegrain, SBIGST7e CCD and AO."

THE SIMPLE LIFE, WITH HEALTH AND SAFETY

"Beware of the scribes, which love... the chief seats in the synagogues and the uppermost rooms at feasts." St Mark's Gospel 12:38, could hardly have foreseen the plight of a Suffragen Bishop of the Church of England who, rather than a palace, is given an ordinary detached house with no room for a chapel.

"For which of you, intending to build a tower, sitteth not down first, and counteth the cost, whether he have enough to finish it?" Good advice there, then, from St. Luke's Gospel 14:28. A nice cheap shed will do for the Bishop's contemplation and it will echo the simplicity of the early Christians who had no cathedrals and stained glass.

Nevertheless, if it is to shelter the public – and there's reasonable room for half a dozen, with the record set at 16 – there are various health and safety regulations about heating and so on. No problem. After rendering unto Caesar that which is Caesar's, the good Bishop can find stillness and prayer in his garden refuge.

50

"You don't get much space as a Bishop."

A MEADOW OF WILD FLOWERS

...just as it was 100 years ago, is a priceless jewel in cool Britannia. From building oil rigs through to community work in Papua New Guinea, via many connections between, Tom has landed on a smallholding which hasn't seen any changes in a century.

The cottage is 300 years old and, during the restoration, whether it is a kitchen cupboard or a five-bar gate, if it is possible to make it, Tom makes it in his shed. The policy is strict: local materials, sustainable development, traditional methods and designs, no negative impact on the environment. Tom believes in the opposite of globalisation; to rely on your local environment makes you respect it and care for it.

He also believes in the opposite of modern farming. They use artificial fertilisers and devote themselves to monoculture. For Tom, biodiversity is what Nature intended and farming should be in tune, not in conflict.

"My neighbour said, you going to plough it, then?"

HISSING SID EATS BATTY BAT

Well, not bats exactly, but mice the snakes certainly eat, and rats, rabbits, guinea pigs, chicks – all bought frozen, plus rainbow trout as a treat for the crocodiles. Stillborn lambs are a hit with the Burmese pythons.

The common iguana normally hangs out in trees overlooking water, into which it will unhesitatingly plunge if disturbed. This one prefers Andy, who also has about 40 pythons in his shed, various other lizards, and a dozen or two venomous cobras of both the striking and the spitting kinds. He has a boa constrictor which was thrown over the wall of an animal rescue centre on a December day, which he has nursed back to full health.

Andy's ambition is to breed his biggest animals, a pair of Asian reticulated pythons. He will use temperature and humidity to imitate their home seasonal cycle, which is quite an art. Then he'll introduce them in their early Spring and hope that a young reticulated python's fancy lightly turns to thoughts of love.

"Do not disturb the iguana."

EVERYWHERE, WE'RE BATTERED BY SOUND

The small, frail, balsa and tissue paper model aeroplane, with its rubber band motor, is launched with a whirr and a slight rattle into the breeze by its nervous maker. To his satisfaction and surprise, the aircraft climbs and, as the twists in the rubber run out, glides slowly back to earth with the sun glinting on its shiny, painted wings.

This mental picture, taken by Gordon when he was thirteen, stayed with him through the years until, retired, he could set about recreating it. His aircraft are bigger now. Some are radio-controlled gliders for slope-soaring. Others have electric motors, powered by batteries for almost silent running.

He doesn't make them too big – six feet wingspan or so – because he likes to take them on holiday in the car. His wife can paint her watercolours while Gordon goes soaring in silence. The quietness matters to him. It's peaceful in his shed, making something that he can watch as it flies without a sound, the sun glinting on its shiny, painted wings...

"There's no noise in a standing wave of air."

YO HO HO AND A BOTTLE OF PINOT NOIR

The base for the shed had already been built by the time they moved to their new house on the Friday morning. The wood arrived on the Friday afternoon and John had the shed shell built by the Sunday. It took him a few more August evenings to do all the fiddly bits but the shed was ready for inaugural ceremonies within the week.

It's a drinking shed, and a theme shed. A beachcombing friend brought a fisherman's net back and the tone was set. Like all theme pubs it is tacky but, in John's case, connoisseurs must appreciate the post-tacky irony with which it is furnished. Friends and family who feature in the list of those privileged to enjoy its facilities bring sea-going treasures back from around the world – a set of shark's teeth, ships in bottles, fancy shells, wall plaques, sea-urchin ash trays, plaster of Paris dioramas of the boy standing on the burning deck, all good stuff like that. And, it doesn't matter if anyone spills a drink because it goes through the floor rather than staining the carpet.

"Have you seen my papier mâché dolphin?"

LET THE SUN SHINE IN

Strictly and formally speaking, the term 'crane' – used because of a resemblance to the bird of that name – refers only to the arm or jib of the mechanism used for lifting heavy weights and displacing them horizontally. Patrick makes that bit out of old bean tins.

By 'crane' we now mean the whole thing, including the cabin, made of papier mâché, and the tracks, made of six dozen cheap 2-inch hinges soldered together. It's a kind of rebirth for Patrick. He used to drive cranes, including the one he's modelling, a 22RB Rushton Bucyrus, the perfect machine renowned throughout the Empire for sand and gravel digging.

Twenty years ago he built his shed, carefully designing it to catch the sun with south-facing, upward tilting windows. He paints it with sump oil every time he gives his car a service then, safe from rot and woodworm, he gets on with his other winter project – recycling bicycles from old wrecks that have been chucked out.

"I make one good 'un out of three."

MAN EMBARRASSES WIFE ON A1

Almost all milkmen say a thankful goodbye to their bottles at the end of their rounds. One who doesn't is Ken. He likes milk bottles so much that he pays good money for them, such as £100 for one of three known examples of the bottle with the actress Zoe Newton pictured on it. Another collector paid £300 for the only one in brown glass.

Ken's collection of about 4,000 bottles, housed in his shed, is small to middling. Some have 10,000, and exchange is good business in Milk Bottle News, a publication yet to feature on BBC2's 'Have I Got News For You' but which boasts a circulation literally over 90. Quality is what matters and Ken's best resource is the Great North Road. He scours the hedge backs for bottles thrown away by lorry drivers of the past. He might find a Blyth Co-op bottle with a 3-colour advert for orange juice. Or he might just embarrass his wife, who sits in the car in the lay-by with her head in the glove box, while Ken does his thing in the ditch.

"Most of my friends are bottle collectors."

63

YOUNG FARMER WAITS PATIENTLY

The Bedford OW short wheelbase tipper, 1944, never got to the war it was built for. Instead it worked for the council, then on a farm in the marshes, and a lad saw its nose sticking out of a barn and offered £25 for it. It was 12 years before truck and money were finally exchanged and Mick could get on with restoration in his shed, itself a war veteran originally meant to house barrage balloons.

Along with his 500cc BSA single pot, his Velocette noddy bike and his Singer Gazelle, the truck is used for fun runs and kept in working order rather than as an untouchable museum piece.

Mick's other passion is growing beef like beef used to be, from proper British breeds. He sells it through his local butcher, where people queue up for the meat the supermarkets won't let them have, which gives him a great deal of satisfaction, along with his vehicles, his organic farming methods, living in the house he was born in, and the old ways.

"It's a lovely place for owls."

POTTING SHED, MAN AND BOY

Michael was a boy potter – five-year apprenticeship at a big pottery firm, £5 a week. He worked his way through to be head thrower in the factory but, after 20 years, with more and more machinery coming in, he began to feel underused.

It became clear that there was no place for a skilled man in a modern pottery factory. A few throwers were kept for display to visitors, but that was all. A shed was the answer, a big shed which used to be part of a bakery, and here he embarked on his mission to defeat the march of the machine. He knew all there was to know about throwing clay but that was all he knew. He had to learn the rest and so, at weekends, he taught himself firing, glazes, putting handles on, all those things.

Michael now has stands at Bakewell market and York and Stratford-on-Avon. Water features, bird feeders, all sorts. All handmade, in his shed.

"The terracotta frog goes down well."

67

THE SHED'S A FINE AND PRIVATE PLACE...

...usually, but here's one which opens to the public. David, smitten by films since he was old enough to watch one, had a personal cinema in the spare room. When they moved house he had to start again, with a new shed, soundproofing, ten seats from the local Odeon, a projection booth and an eight-foot screen.

Every two weeks, a group of OAPs came in for a film show. This was a full programme, with cartoon, tea and biscuits – there will now be a short intermission – everything. Alas, the old 8mm projector was creaking after 20 years and so David went technological. His video projection system produces sound and vision exactly like the old real thing, except you can't hear the clicks.

He gets his 'Coming Shortly' posters from the big cinema when they've finished with them. The OAPs still turn up every fortnight, and his friends from the quiz team. Well, it's not everybody who has a picture house in his garden.

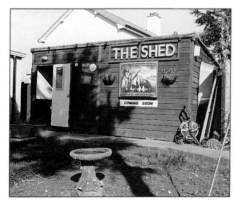

"TV? Films weren't meant for TV."

"I TOLD YOU SO" SAID THE TOAD

The crowd holds its breath as Noah's Ark, the ship built to save the living planet, slides down the slipway. She reaches the water... She's tipping over... She sinks. "I told you it wouldn't float" says a toad spectator, his voice powered by a reprogrammed birthday card insert.

Welcome to Ron's world, the toymaker extraordinaire, who has spent virtually all of his working life in his shed, dreaming up comic fantasies and constructing the intricate means to make them perform. At the moment, lions and marigolds preoccupy his thoughts as he builds an automaton for the local hospital, for the room where children wait for their minor operations.

They'll be able to turn a handle and watch a moth take off from the flowers. The lion follows it with his eyes and goes cross-eyed as it lands on his nose. He sneezes. The moth flits away. The lion tries to catch it, gives up, and the moth settles once more on the marigolds.

"Turn the handle, watch the story."

HE'S GOT THE WHOLE WORLD IN HIS SHED

Does your herd of 150 Fresians need milking? Perhaps you've had a slate or two sucked off your roof by the gale. Possibly a dead elm tree is posing a threat to your upstairs windows, or maybe the windows need new panes of glass, or coats of paint, or the sash weights don't work.

While you are on holiday, your goats/geese/ducks/pigs have to be fed. Winter is drawing near. You must find someone with a tractor and trailer who will cut up the said elm tree for logs. It's spring. The garden needs digging, the new patio needs laying, the washing machine has broken down, the kitchen tap is dripping, the stairwell must be papered, that bit of wall needs rendering and the lawnmower won't start. The septic tank is blocked, the water main is leaking, the chickens need a new hut building, the back field needs fencing, the hay must be baled, the car needs a service, the tumble drier is overheating. For almost any of life's little difficulties, all you need is Eric, chairman, managing director and workforce of Flemco International. One man and his shed.

72

"Me and my shed, O."

I'VE GOT A LUVVERLY BUNCH OF COCONUTS

Dave comes from a long line of travelling showmen and was brought up on the fairgrounds. He and his brother had a set of gallopers (roundabout to you), and a set of dodgems, and overboats. The family home was a caravan for many years until, like so much from the old days, the modern world didn't seem to want them any more.

Dave, now over 80, builds replicas of the showmen's living waggons, much bigger than the gypsy horse-drawn types because they were made to be pulled on good roads by steam traction engine and, later, by lorry. Dave pulls his on a trailer behind his camper van, when he and his wife go to the steam rallies to help raise money for charity.

For those of you watching in black and white, Dave is sitting beside a quarter-size model of his aunt's caravan painted in green, yellow and gold. He's made every little bit of it himself, in his shed.

"We packed it in and went on the tarmacadam."

SIMPLY MADE AND CRUDELY FINISHED

Richard's day job is writing software for palm pilots but he has a genetic compulsion towards his shed. Inheriting a collecting and constructional streak from both grandfathers gives him an irresistible urge to make Pat's crocodile back-pack, John's square and rubbery weekend pants, Wendy's briefcase with stainless steel hawser handles and a coffee table which moves about on three tricycle wheels.

This not so much art trouvé as parts trouvés. He sees a pile of old cylinders, links it with his T-shirt storage problem and conceives the idea of a mild steel wardrobe (see picture). It may look like an enemy of Dr Who but it is a perfectly functional home for Richard's smalls and it has his preferred rough look. Donna's doorknocker, the scary alien's head table and the landing gear chairs are all viewable now at www.jarkman.co.uk. He offers to take on commissions but this would surely mean a potential client having an equal urge, without the constructive skills, towards an office chair with motorcycle shock absorbers or a stereo amplifier with gaspipe and cog. Wouldn't it?

"Anybody want a lunar barbecue?"

WATCHING WALES IN BLACK AND WHITE

Everything in Geraint's personal third of his shed terrace has to be found, not bought. His hermit's cell, therefore, is furnished with a sofa nobody wanted and his TV for watching the rugby is black and white. He admits this can be an advantage if you don't want to see the shirt colour of the team scoring all the tries.

Geraint is a great planner. With three small children he could see his space in the house shrinking and so sketched out his idea of a proper shed, 20 feet long, and took it to the local sawmills. They obliged and so Geraint, a big chap, has the room not to feel squashed. The stone wall is to protect the shed from footballs (what happened to rugby?) when the kids are not in their own third of the shed.

The smallest, third portion, in the middle, is ostensibly for mundanities such as garden tools but was actually designed as a buffer zone. It is fitted with a double forcefield, preventing invasion, which can only be breached by shouting "JPR, where are you now?"

"I wanted something significant in the garden."

SHED MAN CURES VIKING'S DISEASE

In 1964, a young bricklayer called Brian was working alone, cutting some stone with an angle grinder. The machine kicked and sliced almost through his right wrist. Luckily, he was near a hospital and managed to stagger into A&E a moment before he collapsed through loss of blood.

They sewed his hand back on but he spent 30 years, driving HGVs and buses, with two fingers clawed up. Then he developed Dupytren's Contracture (Viking's Disease) in his left hand, all of which clawed up. The large, cumbersome, painful splints used to try to straighten the hand were intolerable and so Brian sat down in his shed and invented a new type. It's small and flexible. It straightens the fingers at rest but allows the hand to grip. Surgeons and occupational therapists all over the world are queuing up. Hospitals in Scandinavia, Germany and the USA are already using it and the rest of the world will follow. There have been great difficulties, with official bureaucracy and sourcing components but Brian has overcome them all. It's amazing what a shed man can do.

"It's a world beater, this is."

GEEZERBIRD IN RED LIGHT DISTRICT

Green musicians in a recording studio like Abbey Road are apt to be struck by Red Light Fever – the inability to perform under the financial and clock-ticking pressure of the dreaded red 'Recording' light.

Phil, well aware of this phenomenon from his own experience, has converted his garden shed into a fully-functioning, fully-equipped, state-of-the-art studio. He offers himself and his gear to the young and talented at modest, non-pressurising fees.

Phil can also offer advice about the long and winding road to musical fame. His own band is Geezerbird, fronted by his singer/songwriter partner who – he says – does geezerish things on rockfaces while he stays home and sees to the ironing. A cross between Blondie and The Eurythmics, they've made their single and their video, they've done the pubs and clubs, Phil's made a dance remix of their song – called, inspirationally, Geezerbird – but stardom knocks not. Yet.

"I love being behind the twiddly buttons."

GED'S ORDINARY SHED

Among this plethora of elaborate sheds and eccentric owners, how refreshing to find someone completely normal. Gerard, known as Ged, has spent his working life surrounded by dozens of other people's children, trying to teach them the difference between King Lear and a dangling participle. Naturally he likes to escape to a small wood and glass box, surrounded by dozens of varieties of deep-rooting and aggressive prairie grasses, where he can sit and consider his next move.

Should he lash out a few quid on six Capsicum F1 Redskin pepper seeds, to grow in pots? He ponders, in his scholarly way, the text on the packet, which pictures a glossy marvel of a plant tumbling with shining red peppers. 'Sunny border or well placed tub' it says. Ged realises that they have accidentally omitted the words 'in Acapulco or Cyprus'. So, what will happen? Sow six seeds, four show, one nibbled by snail, plant three in pots, blackbird pulls one up, remaining two die from sheer misery one cold afternoon or wither because he forgot to water them. No, Ged thinks, he'll leave that for now.

"Say it with vegetables."

LOVE AT FIRST SIGHT

There they were, Chris and his wife, having a normal day out, when a vision of loveliness went past. He fell immediately, truly, madly, deeply. She was also enthusiastic. So it was that they made a promise to each other. One day, when they settled down and had a garden big enough, they would have an old British Railways guard's van as a shed.

The idea is one thing. Obtaining a decrepit 1956 Darlington guard's van is quite another, not to mention building a platform for it to stand on, finding and fixing railway lines and sleepers, paving the lawn with planks so the 50-ton crane can go there to lift the van into the garden through a gap where a row of trees used to be, and restoring it. The right sort of wood came out of a Victorian coach. The paint is the proper stuff in BR Freight Brown. The pot-bellied stove and chimney are precise replicas. It's nearly finished. They both think it's great. The children are going to have sleep-outs in it.

"Barbecue. In guard's van if wet."

IS THAT WHAT THEY'RE FOR?

You have a large, two-level apartment for several modern, young, busy, artistic metropolitans to share. Downstairs are the living quarters where folk that pass in the night and morning can briefly nod their acquaintance. Facilities here are much as might be expected: jacuzzi, potato peeler, toasting fork, coal scuttle, flight simulator, dolly tub, bread-making machine, recordings of steam trains going up the Lickey Incline. Some of that may not be quite right but you know the sort of thing.

The difficulty arises above. It's open plan. Modern metropolitans cavil at dorm living, so what do they do? They tried partitions. Room dividers don't transpose to the average warehouse floor. Luke, visiting a certain well known DIY store in search of jacuzzi powder, had a Damascene experience. There, before him, in cedar and creosote, were things of beauty which also offered him the practical solution to the privacy problem. "You got a big garden, then?" asked the lady at the store. "No" said Luke. "You got lots of small gardens, then?" she said. "No" said Luke.

"They're for upstairs."

A PLACE TO DREAM A BIT

Derek's shed was originally used to keep chickens and goats. Now it's home to a number of his projects – the fruits of a wonderful imagination and a long career as a mechanical design engineer. The fin-shaped device is his safe alternative to a conventional propeller: it works in an up-and-down motion, like a fish's tail.

His affinity with sheds goes back some way. During the '70s, he was part of a team that developed a pedal-powered aeroplane. It could be dismantled to fit through a standard 30-inch-wide door, but it had a 136 foot wingspan, and they had nowhere to keep it, until some bright spark hit on the idea of erecting two pre-fabs end-to-end and knocking through.

Derek's latest set-up is a bit more permanent, though his design work has had to take second place to maintenance. "I spent most of last winter positioning buckets to catch the drips through the roof. It's still coming into the house, but I think I've got the shed sorted."

"Most of the firms I worked for went bust."

THE SECRET OF A SUCCESSFUL MARRIAGE

For Bryan, a shared interest is the key. "If your wife disagrees with the thing you like most, it wouldn't work. You've got to do it together..." As Bryan's model railway takes up the whole garden, it's good that his wife Sandra is happy for him to maintain the tracks and rolling stock while she looks after the flowers, which tower like triffids over the passengers on the platforms. "You do have your ups and downs... Like when a train hits one of her plants and runs off the tracks." Come rain or shine they're out there, even during the winter months. And there's no such thing as the wrong kind of snow – Bryan has a concrete-laden plough to clear the rails.

His shed's the hub of the operation. It's the control room and contains all the tools he needs for repairs, plus a regiment of old Brylcreem pots, which contain "proper" sheddy stuff like nails and screws. "What I really could've done with is a bigger shed – a two-tier job with the track running around the bottom and the operating side in the top half... I don't think I could have got planning permission – it'd be 20 foot high."

"You get married to your shed as well."

AN EVENING AT GUZZLE-DOWN LODGE

In its previous incarnation, Guzzle-Down Lodge was a summerhouse – one half functioning as a kid's playhouse, the other side as an aviary. It wasn't getting used a great deal, apart from Ken (with mic) and others – like brother Lol, Doug and Colin – sitting around the table. Ken would find himself traipsing back to the house for fresh supplies every few minutes; a "little brainwave" led him to install a bar in the corner.

"It sort of went from one extreme to the other," he says, sheepishly. The hostelry now boasts lasers, smoke machine, disco lights, two-screen karaoke machine… oh, and beer on tap. Car-boot purchases and gifts from the regulars have provided visual interest: a plaque his wife bought him even inspired the name.

Aside from special occasions, such as the annual New Year's Eve bash and the family lunch on Christmas Day, Ken now plays host and MC roughly once a month. "We have music till about 11 o'clock and then everyone starts screaming for karaoke… That normally finishes about 4 o'clock in the morning."

"It's got everything that a nightclub's got, really."

95

THE BEST CURRACH HOUSE IN TOWN

Holger was involved in collaborative research between the Eden project and Falmouth College of Art, examining traditional crafts and sustainable plant materials, and bringing those elements into architecture. He found inspiration in the Irish currach – a mode of water transport similar to the coracle. "The boat is like a container when you're on the water. But on land you'd turn it around and then it's like a shelter."

Taking this traditional craft, he added a pinch of modern architecture, incorporating a row of windows beneath the roof, and elements that open up to let the light in and compensate for the dark materials the shed is made from. "The roof is made from woven hazel rods, like a Boyne river currach. The rest of the shed is made of willow rods, changing the design a little bit."

Holger gave it to Katie and Sara, a ceramic designer and a photographer. The pair have given it a particularly fitting home – an allotment close to the sea. "It looks great. Sitting on the hill, it really sticks out."

"All the other sheds are ordinary, little, rough-looking thingies."

TONY'S TIGER SHED

Tony's garden shed is a museum dedicated to tiger artefacts amassed from countries across the world. Everyone he knows is on the look-out for tigers wherever they go. His daughter is particularly good at tracking them down. "She travels a lot and always has her eye open."

Sitting whisker by jowl alongside Guatemalan figurines, Mexican masks and Japanese clockwork models are a number of pieces Tony has commissioned from local artists. He even has a 9-foot long fibreglass tiger from the Bridgwater Festival. "We stuck it in the car and I had to lie horizontal with the tiger in the front seat as we drove along the motorway… It caused quite a few raised eyebrows."

Tony's wife is involved with local education and they have parties of school children round to visit. A trail of tiger footprints leads them from the road over walls and dustbins to the shed. "The teacher then sits on the tiger chair and reads the children a story while they wear the little tiger tails my wife makes for them."

"I don't collect cuddly toys."

AS TIME WHIPS BY

James discovered the joy of metal at the tender age of 14. On his first day as an engineer he was put to work on a lathe and the rest just followed. "I've enjoyed my life as an engineer. I look back and I've been paid for a pleasure."

James enjoyed it so much, in fact, that he'd soon built himself a shed and kitted it out with all the tools an engineer could need, making as much of the machinery as he could with a blend of scrap metal and love. Word soon got around and he became the street's knife sharpener and car mechanic. "I found if you do something for free you were always passed on to someone else."

He made toys for the children – jigsaws, dolls' houses, even a go-kart modelled on a Rolls Royce. Recent projects include a tune-playing scale-model barrel organ and a fully working mini spinning wheel, as well as paintings and poems. "As I'm working my mind sort of wanders... The only thing is that time just whips by."

"I've tried to spin on it but it's too small."

SHED DELAYS MILLION-METRE-CLUB MEMBERSHIP

The old shed collapsed. Gordon's wife needed "somewhere to put the mower where it won't get wet." Soon afterwards, on a trip to review and photograph a jazz festival in the States, he came across what's known over there as a "backyard barn". Inspired, he tracked down plans on the internet, only to discover that across the pond they still use imperial measurements and have their own terminology for things like nails.

But, determined as he was, he put all his energies into it for six weeks, even putting off his goal of reaching a million metres on his indoor rower. "If you reach a million, they send you a free T-shirt." He even adapted the plans to incorporate a secret entrance at the back for his granddaughters, India and Mali. "It's 3 foot high and opens up on to the trees at the back of our garden."

So everyone was happy? "My wife's comment at the end of it all was, 'It's too good. I'm not sure I can put a mower in there.'"

"They measure nails not by size but by how many you got for a penny 100 years ago."

A SHEDMAN AMONG SHEDMEN

When John's first poetry collection, "The Nutter in the Shrubbery" was published, he had no idea that just months later he would be running school workshops and performing at festivals as his alter-ego Shedman…

It all began when he entered an Arts Council competition for a placement in a place of architectural interest. A fan of Brighton's Booth Museum, John discovered that it was classed as both a listed building and a shed, because it originally stood next to the Booth family home. And so, he suggested he'd work in a shed within Booth's shed. Needless to say he won, and soon found himself stacked out with people coming to see him.

Requests for Shedman's services followed and he has since performed everywhere from a quayside to a school library. "It was a boy's school, and the teachers were amazed because I actually got the kids writing." John thinks he might be getting a bit obsessed. A shed even features in his audio-book for children "Dangerous Territory", the story of a disabled lad trying to save his pet llamas.

"The next thing is for me to live in the shed for two weeks."

A SHED IN PROGRESS

Dave started off with a vacant allotment plot and a vague idea of what he wanted his allotment shed to look like. "That's the starting point for everything – the shed." But so many friends got involved that he found the design changing day by day... "Everybody had their input."

His original idea was to have a large veranda on the shed and a bit of decking to sit out on. Now the plan is to have a herb and veg garden to the left, and to the right a decked area, gazebo, chair swing and industrial-sized barbecue to keep the troops, like Peter and Craig here, entertained throughout the summer months.

Dave confesses he isn't particularly green-fingered – "I'm absolutely numb at growing. I don't know anything." But the main objective is leisure, and the trading of traffic for wildlife, exhaust fumes for fresh air. The rest he's learning as he goes. "One guy's motto is 'Just make sure you've got somewhere to keep the beer cold.'" Dave's got a big cool box... "That'll be a feature at some point."

"The beer will probably get in the way in the summer."

BRIAN'S LOFT CONVERSION

A nine-year-old Brian was asked to look after his young mate's pigeons when he went on holiday. It was the beginning of a love affair that is still going strong half a century on. These days, Brian is at the top of his field, with regular success in National Flying Club races, and an expert on the science behind the sport. "I can predict it more now. I can tell what a pigeon is in terms of whether its character will do 500 miles or whether its character will do 700. And there is a big difference."

Breeding is crucial to success, but then there's training and diet – "Maize for sprints, peanuts for the longer distance" – and the pigeons' very own Olympic village. The loft-shed would cost a small fortune in London. Brian designed the mock-Tudor façade on the principle that light colours reflect the sun and keep the interior cool, and also on the principle that blending it in with the surrounding architecture would keep the neighbours happy. For really hot days, the ceiling moves to regulate the temperature...

"It's the working man's horse-racing."

THE SHED AT THE END OF THE ROAD

It's a common occurrence in smaller villages for one person to combine a number of trades as there is less demand for one particular service. Peter, owner of Langmaid & Hunking, is the local builder-cum-undertaker, and runs the business from a two-storey, former fisherman's shed. "There's not enough work to do funeral directing all the time. I normally do about 15 to 20 funerals a year."

Peter has been with the company for 25 years and can still remember his first undertaking in the world of undertaking. "It was certainly a bit nerve-racking the first time Mr Langmaid said to me that somebody had died in the village and would I be able to go up with him and lend a hand."

They used to get the wood from a nearby mill and build the coffins in the shed. These days, however, Peter orders in the coffin shells and fits them out with the lining and furniture. But what remains is the personal touch. "It makes a difference to people that I'm local, that they know me."

"I'm there 20 minutes doing the job, and then for another hour talking about the person."

GONNA START A REVOLUTION FROM MY SHED

At the shed-quarters of Cappella Archive, David is waging a war on inferior paper and binding, and the waste of over-printing. "Modern printing techniques allow books to be printed one at a time, as they are ordered." He uses his own "print on demand" system, which means he can produce quality editions in-house, one at a time, hundreds of times faster than the average person can read them.

In a former life he was an A–level teacher and, after years of "trying to set damp students alight on the hearth of English Literature", he took early retirement to pursue his passion for books in a more physical manner. The shed has been his base since the early days, as he wasn't allowed to keep the machines in the house.

All of the books he produces are commissioned, such as historical reproductions for local bookshops; some are more unusual, like the anglicised version of a French novel about Jack the Ripper, first published in 1935. "We had to pay £200 for a rather tatty paperback, which we then translated."

"We do everything from the printing to the cloth binding."

THE DRINK AND DREAM TEA-SHED

Tony's had an eye for follies since he was a young lad, particularly 18th-century ones with an oriental flavour. He was so inspired by them that it was only a matter of time until he brought one home.

One seemingly normal day, Tony was dutifully clearing brambles from the bottom of the garden, while trying to think up a special present for his wife's birthday. Having finally bagged up the mess, he had a sheddist epiphany – here at last, was a teahouse-sized space. So, with room and reason enough, he enlisted the help of a friend to make his long-held dream a reality.

Like Tony, the shed's not just a pretty face. Take the mural on the back wall, for example: Tony's an Englishman, his wife's Danish – so he painted the English and Danish delegations, which stand side by side in Canton, flying the countries' national flags. Then there's the way he located the shed so that it suddenly creeps up on you three quarters of the way down the garden. "It's a nice surprise in an 18th century way."

114

"It should really have water around it, but the ditch is still undug."

PENNY'S ROYAL TEA

"The first thing blokes on an allotment need is a shed. It's where you brew up and have your meetings and that." So says Ken, who can always be found on his local plot, followed closely by Penny, faithful pooch and top-notch ratter.

The shed is home to his tools and seeds for next year's plants, plus an array of cards and certificates from numerous shows – recognition of 40-odd years' worth of growing chrysanthemums and dahlias, not to mention sweet peas, swedes, onions and leeks, turnips and tomatoes… "I can supply myself for the year with the stuff I grow. There's nowt like pulling your own veg out of the ground."

And if he's not working the plot he'll most likely be in the shed, frying up a hearty meal of bacon and eggs on the stove or brewing a cuppa for one of his visitors – and Penny, of course: "If anybody comes and I make them a cup of tea, I have to make her one too. She won't be left out."

"It keeps me going – I love it."

THE REAL STRING SHEDDY

For years, Andy was a joiner by day, a musician by night. A self-confessed "wood and guitar junkie", these days he combines his two passions – making and repairing guitars in his beloved shed. "Well, you can't go cutting up wood in the front room. And a shed gives you that freedom where you can go and have your bits strewn everywhere without getting whinged at."

Andy built the shed to fit his exacting requirements and applies this rule-of-thumb to the instruments he creates: "If you want a certain look of one with a bit of another, you basically take three or four different types and make up one you'd like." He also gets the odd unusual request, including one where someone asked him to put frets on a violin. "Your purist would freak out."

Above and beyond all that, Andy's shed is his "nice retreat", his home-from-home. "Though I don't have the makings for tea and coffee in the shed – I have to go down the house for that."

"You've got to have a shed."

THE VIEW FROM THE WITCHHOUSE

When the original witchhouse was built in the mid-1700s, the then owner of Hestercombe House in Somerset – one Coplestone Warre Bampfylde – was creating a fantasy garden. He decided he wanted a special garden building with a seat from which to gaze at the central water-feature – a 50-foot waterfall called the Great Cascade – and witches and grottoes were all the rage... so he settled on a "witchhouse". "It was nothing to do with black magic," says Philip. "It was just a bit of fun."

The magic came later. By the 1990s, the witchhouse and the garden were all but forgotten, swallowed up by time and densely overgrown woodland. It was Philip's chance discovery of the hidden garden that set him on the long and arduous path of restoration. As for the witchhouse, it may never have been rebuilt, had someone not rolled up at Hestercombe one day with a magazine from 1906, which featured a photograph of the mysterious building. Armed with the photograph and a description from 1761, Philip and co. were able to find the exact spot where the original witchhouse stood. The rest is history.

120

"Children just love it."

A SHEDFUL OF HISTORY

Nick's love affair with the soda siphon began with a red, teardrop-shaped gem he found in a charity shop. "The attraction was in the design – there's that law of aesthetics where anything designed to be maximally efficient is also beautiful." He also feels a desire to preserve a little bit of social heritage, a principle which applies equally to his other collections, ranging from sweet wrappers to products from the Pifco factory.

His collections featured in a reality TV show in which a team of experts "de-clutter" your house. "We walked in with our eyes closed – the classic set-up. When we opened them, everything was lovely and empty…" But when the cameras stopped rolling, it transpired that the crew had 25 full boxes in the van outside.

So he got a shed. A right beauty she is too – maximal *and* efficient. He's even lined it to keep things nice and cosy in winter. But a shed can only offer so much help. "The theory is that every time I go to a collectors' fair, I sell. But when I go to a car boot, I end up buying again, although the ratio is much better than it was."

**"It was taking up the bedroom.
It was a bit embarrassing really."**

...OH, AND HOW'S THE SHED?

Dave moved into his house just over two years ago. Imagine his dismay when he turned up in his removal van, only to discover that the previous owners had taken the shed with them. After the initial palpitations, he resolved to purchase a replacement forthwith.

Friends and family took great interest in his impending shed purchase. "It's all I heard for months. They weren't saying, 'How're you settling in?' but, 'Have you got your shed yet?'" And then, once he'd installed the shed, the same people would "Pop round for a cup of tea" just to see it...

It wasn't all bad though – one kind friend gave him a spider plant: "It was an offcut of their own. It's called Boris – technically the one I've got is Boris II." Boris II now sits happily in the shed, adding a bit of greenery to Dave's otherwise minimalist haven. "It's my place to get away from it all and relax, though it's a bit ironic really as I live on my own. It's nice to not have a telly or telephone or anything in here."

"I chose it from scratch."

A PAIR OF ORTHODOX SHEDS

Five years ago, Stephen left the Church of England in order to set up a Centre for Orthodox Mission with three other like-minded people, which they named the Community of St Fursey, after the Apostle of Norfolk.

Due to a reduced income, Stephen could only afford an end-terrace house with a small garden. As the group wanted to use the house as a retreat centre, they needed a chapel for the services and a library to house a large collection of religious works for the visitors to read and study. Sheds were the only answer.

The beautiful shed chapel came first – carefully modelled on a 4th-century Roman church in Silchester – and is commonly referred to as "Stephen's Byzantine Shed". The library shed followed, and is now a hive of activity, with Stephen making religious icons and producing newsletters for local market stalls. And, as it's warm and cosy, it has also become the obvious place to hold the weekly bible study. "In fact, when our priest comes, he prefers to go in there rather than in the house – he finds it more comfortable."

126

"It's a mini-basilica."

THE RETIRING TYPE

Some people dream of retiring somewhere hot, others want a bit of peace and quiet. Tony wanted both. A computing communications manager for a large company, he found his job getting increasingly stressful as his team was gradually whittled away. He wasn't happy, so he made plans and got out when he could.

Tony now divides his leisure time between charity work, volunteering on the Bala Lake railway and his shed, where he makes beautifully-painted wooden cartoon characters – from the small ones you see here right up to 6-foot-plus monsters – in addition to toys and the occasional less fun, practical object, like a bookcase. It keeps him happy and makes a lot of other people happy too. "I'm like a tortoise," he says. "My shed's somewhere I can go and shrink into my shell."

But, unlike a tortoise, he avoids the need for hibernation by spending the winter months in his other shed in Florida. "I do the same thing out there. Though they like wooden palm trees."

"I planned my retirement about 20 years before I retired."

YOU NAME IT, HE'S GOT IT

Some 19 years ago, Frank and family bought a derelict farm complete with barn and cowsheds and set about turning the outhouses into a place to display a lifetime's worth of collections. "We used to live in a little bungalow, and I put sheds up in the garden to store it all in. The spare rooms were full and I had to climb over stuff to get in the bed."

Walton House Museum has now been open to the public for 11 years. Each of his eight different sheds has its own theme, like "1940s kitchen" or "printing works". "We've got military, motoring, household, Victorian, nursery, dairy..." His current favourite is his collection of over 50 road rollers. He sources them from around the country, rejuvenating them with parts made in his blacksmith's shed, such as cast iron name-plates.

Frank hopes the grandkids will take on the museum one day. "I've got a couple of them really interested." Granddaughter Jade even has her own roller, won in a Road Roller Association competition. He's very proud.

"It's like my own little village."

131

A SHEDI KNIGHT

For Adrian, reading about the past simply isn't enough. He'd much rather head down to his garden shed, choose a costume and set out to do battle for the Red Wyverns historical re-enactment group and the Clifford household: "They were prominent and interesting players in the War of the Roses."

But re-enactment only goes so far. John "Butcher" Clifford would find the rules for fighting – such as no head shots – a bit restrictive. "It's probably not as dangerous as rugby, but there are risks." And not everyone gets involved in the fighting – in fact, it's a family-based activity, with an emphasis on "living history" demonstrations. Participants can choose from a range of contemporary characters, from monks to peasants to jesters, and engage in traditional activities, from cooking to leatherworking to basket-weaving.

As well as being a communal store, Adrian's shed functions as a workshop for repairing armour and making arrows. And, when he's not kitted up or fixing up kit, he's working on their website, www.red-wyverns.co.uk.

"When we first started doing it all my stuff fitted in a bag."

133

BETWEEN A TREE AND A HARD PLACE

Chris and Nick have always shared a shed fascination – as boys they curtained off half of Nick's dad's shed to create a unique meeting place: "Many a winter's evening was spent huddled around an old oil lamp."

In adulthood, then, Chris was never truly satisfied with a plain 8 x 6 foot shed, so began work on his own designs. There were two problems with his garden, though – a huge bank of stone and the tree his grandmother Rose had planted 35 years ago. The first problem he solved with a trailer and six weeks of graft: his parents got a new rockery and he got the garden's full width. Now all he had to do was decide: the shed he really wanted… or the tree.

"There was no way I could cut it down. The only solution was to re-design the shed." And with help from mates Melvyn, Gary, Dave and Nick, and refreshments from fiancée, Beryl, the drawing became reality, hastening a return to the shed, 40 years on, to discuss life over coffee and roll-ups.

"Bliss."

135

PEOPLE IN GRASS HOUSES...

Gary and his girlfriend wanted a garden workshop but they needed to keep costs down. Gary was reading a book on eco-design, which featured a number of buildings with turfed roofs... "And what could be cheaper than a few planks, a bit of boarding and some soil from the garden?"

By the time it became apparent that it was going to be both more complex and expensive, it had become a challenge. The shed was initially planned as a light wooden structure but is now much more like a bunker. "I did think about putting some camouflage netting on it but I'm not sure how that'll go down."

He hasn't had to trim the grass yet. "I bought seed that said on it, 'Resists Birds'. Basically that was a lie. It was bird *food*." But then the cat began to use the roof as a bed. This got rid of the birds but the cat created its own mess, so Gary doused the turf in cat repellent. "The problem is I hate the stuff. It's keeping me away from the shed too."

"I'm not going up there every couple of weeks with the mower..."

THE LURE OF THE SEA

Jim's father and grandfather were shrimp fishermen but, being his own man, he became an engineer. Over the years, however, he found himself drawn back to the coastal waters of his youth and the family business.

The training came in handy too. In the quest to trawl ever deeper for the tasty little crustaceans, Jim helped turn an ex-Army four-wheel-drive wagon into the Daddy of all shrimping vessels – a prototype for the vehicle he is using today. Similarly, when he set up Southport Potted Shrimps with wife Elizabeth in 1980, he applied his analytical skills to developing their own recipe. "I went around buying up all the potted shrimps I could find and I didn't like any of them." So he took the original mid-19th-century recipe and developed it to please his own tastebuds.

The shed – now the company HQ – came later, the awards and commendations soon after that. In fact, demand's grown so much that Jim's developing the dot.com side of things – see www.pottedshrimp.co.uk.

"They're lovely on toast."

"TO ME, IT'S JUST SOMETHING I'VE DONE...

"...But to other people, it's something unusual." So says David, who's "just" transforming his shed into a narrowboat – well the inside, anyway. Every possible bit of space is decorated: the walls are embellished, painted pots and pans hang from the ceiling, even the furniture he works on has already been worked on.

As a boy, he would watch his grandfather painting the gypsy caravan they shared. This fond memory was kindled by trips on the canal years later, inspiring him to learn the craft himself. The idea for his shed came to David while he was convalescing after a triple heart bypass. "It switches me right off from everything. Until I hear a voice say, 'Dinner's ready.' And then I'm in quick, I might tell you."

It's made him quite a few friends. "I live in a sheltered block. Some of the ladies come along to visit, and Flo, my missus, says, 'Hello, you're in there with a woman.' Then my neighbour up the top, every day he says, 'I've got to come down to see your shed.' He's been here for a year but he's still amazed what he sees."

"Of course when the weather's good the missus wants me to take her out."

HOLY HERRINGBOAT, SHEDMAN!

The history of herring fishing on Lindisfarne goes back almost as far as Christianity. And, just as without Christ there would be none of the island's glorious religious monuments, without the humble herring there would be none of its awe-inspiring boatsheds, like the one George is fortunate enough to look after.

Relics to a former way of life on the Holy Island, the majority of the boats are now put to use as worksheds and places to store fishing equipment and "other stuff". "The bulk of the fishing finished before the first world war," George says. "My grandmother told me that, as a child, she could run along the tops of the herring barrels from what we call the Steel End to the Castle Point, which must be well over a mile."

The exact origins of the boatsheds are vague. It's not known whether the bloke who started it all had some kind of artistic vision or was simply looking for a way of putting his leaky old vessel to practical use. Either way, George is a very lucky man.

"I've got two other sheds, a old coal house, two very big lofts, and a cellar – all bunged full."

FOR THOSE OF YOU WATCHING IN BLACK AND WHITE

A shed usually precedes its contents, but not in the case of Crucible II. Says Martin, "A local college were refurbishing the staff room and selling the snooker table. It was such a reasonable price I just had to buy it." The table was stored first in the garage, then the attic, then the sitting room – "much to my wife's protest." After briefly considering an extension, they decided on a shed and set about consulting neighbours, checking with the relevant authorities and finding someone local to build the 30 x 24 foot timber structure…

Now it's up, wife and mum Maria reads the papers on the verandah and cat Faith sits on the ridge of the roof, while Martin and Dom put in a few hours of practice for the weekend when Dom plays at a club in Aldershot and competes in regional tournaments. With a handicap of 55 and a top break of 51, he's a prodigious talent. Dad's current best of 29 doesn't quite put him in the same class, but Crucible II has certainly rekindled his interest. "I've even decided that I might enter a few competitions."

144

"I'm accused of being a bit of a Cliff Thorburn."

MY OTHER SHED'S A MERCEDES

There's probably a correlation between the structures most men are wont to build as lads – dens, bivouacs and such like – and the sheds they go on to own in later life.

Alan – a young pup by sheddist standards – and his "bender" sit somewhere between these two states. He built the skeleton of the structure from a load of willow branches a mate had lying around in his garage. His mate's father was happy to have the branches out of the way but apparently is still looking for the tarpaulin.

Initially, the bender caused a bit of a stir on the allotment, but natural friendliness overcame a couple of the regulars who stopped for a chat. "One or two came up and said, 'Hmm that's quite interesting… What is it?'" Alan prefers its "organic" appearance to your common-or-gardener allotment shed. Similarly, in the midst of order, he opts for a *laissez-faire* approach. "Most of the plots are square and regimental but mine's a bit more relaxed."

146

"I do a fair bit of weeding."

THE SHED IS DEAD, LONG LIVE THE SHED

Standing like a sentinel by a stretch of windswept estuary, this towering work of beauty is the result of a collaboration between Wilf and Tony, architect and artist, respectively. "We're very proud of it as it's one of the largest public art pieces in the area, and it's much loved and visited."

Most of the visitors are keen birders who love the range of vision the 10-metre height provides them with. "The budget was only for something about 10–15 feet, but Wilf managed to persuade them that they needed something really substantial." The pair also took the boredom threshold of children into account, including little surprises for them to discover, like the dinosaur-sized wooden egg nestled inside the building.

The shed is truly wildlife-friendly, with design features such as a double-roof made of cedar – to encourage the attentions of the local bird populace. A bird even featured in the opening ceremony: the centrepiece was a huge phoenix Tony sculpted from pieces of the old shed, which they lit on the night as a symbol of renewal.

148

"We got a construction team to do all the dangerous stuff."

A SEAT IN THE ROYAL BOX

Welcome to The Regal, John's very own shed-cinema, where performances are held throughout the winter months to the delight of nine lucky, lucky friends. And it's a truly authentic experience – with seats and signs from Letchworth's deceased Broadway Cinema, a box office and projection room, a programme list, forever frozen in 1959, and various bits of cinema memorabilia, including a life-sized cardboard Mrs Doubtfire...

Peggy, John's long-suffering wife, visits during the brief intermission, clad in full usherette garb and conveying refreshments for all in attendance. John places the orders via the "intercom" – a baby alarm he picked up from a junk shop and appropriated. "She doesn't mind – it's all part of the fun."

A self-confessed film-lover, there is one movie John cannot stand: *The Sound of Music*. Recently, however, he found a second-hand copy and, having moaned so much about it, decided to buy it for a laugh. "It was only ten quid, so I thought why not. But I've only got as far as Julie running up the hill at the start."

150

**"Peggy puts up with a lot.
I'm a little bit eccentric."**

151

THE NEXT BIG SHED

Pete had just completed a music qualification. He was desperate to chase his dream of having his own studio, plus his drumming was annoying the neighbours – "Not the neighbours, but the next-door-but-one."

And so, he took what was a connected greenhouse and summerhouse, and set about converting it into a fully sound-proofed recording studio. It took 4 tonnes of sand for the walls and a tonne of concrete for the roof. As for the doors, "I made the framework out of three by two and then filled it full of concrete and left it to dry. I had trouble getting it in. It must've weighed 400 pounds."

Things developed from there. "I've done all sorts from rehearsals – teenagers starting out with their bands – to a string section on a heavy metal album." And it's not all hard work – he sets up the odd barbecue-cum-gig on the raised patio outside. His dad provides freshly-caught trout to chuck on the coals and they get a few mates round... "Now we've got a toilet shed to save people going in and out of the house."

"The next-door neighbours quite liked our band really."

THE SHED THAT TIME FORGOT

Just over 2,000 years ago – before Roman invaders had set foot on British soil – roundhouses like this one could be found up and down the country. The allotment on which Paul is reconstructing it has yielded fragments of Iron Age pottery and flints from the late Neolithic, and there's archaeological evidence of a fishing community and a roundhouse settlement nearby.

With the help of family and friends, Paul cleared a derelict plot and built the structure with locally-sourced materials, which would have been used originally, such as oak, willow and hazel, and began growing Iron Age crops like leeks, beans, wheatstraw, woad and flax around it. The shed even had an authentic turf roof, but keeping it dry to prevent it collapsing finally proved too much, and Paul decided to thatch it.

The aim is to invite students from schools and colleges to come down, see how our ancestors lived and learn about ceramics and metalwork technologies from the era. "It'll be like visiting a farm 2,500 years ago."

"It wasn't fun going down to light a fire in the middle of the night."

EVERY STOP I MAKE, I MAKE A NEW SHED

It's a tradition with Chris that, when he moves house, he puts up a new shed. An experienced potter, Chris uses this – shed number four – to explore a number of Chinese glazes, whilst working with a wide range of domestic-ware, stoneware and porcelain, plus floor tiles with medieval designs. He likes the idea of combining "old materials and new materials, old ideas and new ideas", a principle he's applied as much to the shed as to his craft.

The shed's certainly unique. The old materials he's used include two 19th-century stained-glass windows from a knocked down church plus 1930s doors and windows from local houses that went double-glazed. The overall design has a Georgian flavour – testament to his favourite architecture; the roof looks like an upturned boat – he used to be a boat-builder; and the verandah is borrowed straight from South Carolina – "It's perfect for a late evening beer, sitting on the rocking chair and listening to the abundant wildlife." You can almost imagine the sound of cicadas chirruping in the sunset.

"I build the biggest one I can get away with."

THE SHED MENAGERIE

Ralph's been keeping guinea pigs on and off for 40 years. He's had as many as 200 in the past, owing to their tendency to reproduce, but these days he keeps a more modest brood of seven in his allotment shed. The cast of characters includes Dennis the Menace and the Bad Lads. "The Bad Lads are brothers. They were a pair of little so-and-sos, and they automatically became The Bad Lads."

Dennis and co. share their living space with rabbits and pigeons, but at 81 feet long, the shed affords them ample room. As the shed stands 2 feet off the ground, it also protects them from the occasional floods of rainwater and sewage that blight the allotments after downpours.

Ralph has the slightly smaller "tea shed" next door. "You get the fire going and everybody turns up." There are no further sheds in the pipeline though. "I've finished expanding now – there's no more room. Between the sheds, the two greenhouses and the chicken shed, you have to grow a certain amount of vegetables."

"They're the best pets a kid could have."

A FAMILY TREEHOUSE

Martin's grandkids loved playing in the wood and the river he's lucky enough to have in his back garden. They wanted to play in the trees too, so he installed a two-storey tree-shed, complete with bunk beds, water and electricity, connected to platforms in other trees by rope bridges, which overlook the river. "We build boats and have races – HMS Grandad and HMS Oliver." The tree-shed looks like something out of a fairytale, and not surprisingly the grandkids love it almost as much as Martin.

Selling up his business a few years back, he now devotes his energies to the things that matter most to him – the family and his charity. And so, when the kids aren't visiting, he can probably be found researching the family genealogy, or working on behalf of the Zambian Lubwe project (see www.lubwe-hospital.org.uk).

It all takes up rather a lot of time. Between Zambia, the family tree and the grandkids, there just aren't enough hours in the day.

"Probably their biggest passion is throwing stones in the river."

"I'VE NEVER BEEN BORED IN MY LIFE"

There are blacksmiths and then there are fabricators – lesser-skilled tradesmen who simply take mass-produced components and weld them together. Steve, the brains and brawn behind Ironshed (www.ironshed.co.uk), is passionately of the former category. "As you drive around you'll see a lot of hideous gates, and they're probably the same the country over. When you see a blacksmith's work, you can identify it from certain flourishes – it's like a signature."

For years, Steve divided his time between his day job and his band. While the music's still there in the background, he now gets his kicks from metal of a physical kind: "In the morning, I go outside to the shed and it's just a load of flat strips. By the evening something exists. It's very tangible, what you've achieved."

Steve also teaches, has a recording studio, is into motorbikes and has recently taken up flying microlight aircraft… "Life's just a little bit on the short side to fit it all in."

"I've had a crack at most hobbies in my time."

I LOVE THE SMELL OF TEAK IN THE MORNING

"It takes me right back to my school days and working on the lathe, and into my own shed there." But it's not just the smell of the wood that holds such memories for Stuart: it's the feel, the shine, the colour of the grain and the process of crafting objects of use and beauty, be they bowls or walking sticks, or the stools he once fashioned from two old beer barrels.

He's had a passion for wood and sheds since the tender age of 14, when he added an 8-foot extension to his father's shed, which itself had been built by his grandfather. He ran power out to the building, and acquired a woodworking bench that he still uses today.

And it seems that Stuart's sheddist tendencies have been passed down. "My son will go in and use the tools and all the rest of it, and now my eldest grandson, Tom, has started. He was there last Sunday, and he said, 'Granddad, what are we going to make?'"

"If he gets a shed, he'll be a fifth generation sheddist."

"WHAT'S THE POINT OF DOING EASY THINGS?"

Science is primarily based on the idea of taking things to bits in order to understand them, technology on building a machine to do a certain task. Steve's work in the field of artificial intelligence is slightly different. "I'm trying to understand the brain by building one. I'm taking an engineer's approach to science."

Three years ago, he set himself up in his shed and began work on Lucy the robot, and has since begun making a more efficient version of her – Lucy 2 – with the help of Lottery funding. As Lucy is based on an orangutan, she has already learnt to recognize bananas and Steve says she has attained the intelligence level of a frog.

Her organs are fairly straightforward – her eye is a TV camera, for example – but the brain is a bit more complicated. As making biological nerve cells is currently beyond science and transistors are nothing like nerve cells, Steve has had to create cells virtually – inside a computer. "Then you have to try and figure out how to put those neurons together in ways that can learn to think – and that's the tricky bit."

"It's hard to be intelligent when you're built out of junk."

THE REASON THE PUBS ARE EMPTY

Rick, John and Peter love their local… The beer's cheap and plentiful, there are no crowds at the bar and no last orders bell, they get to choose what music is played and what match gets shown on the television, there's no dress code, no smoking, no trouble and the comfy seat is always free.

They've been meeting in Rick's shed – the 179 Club – for seven years now. It was a humble 10 x 8 foot job, to which he added three old double-glazed windows to the front to get a bit of light in and a mirror on the back wall… "It makes the place look a bit bigger." He then hooked up a TV aerial to the side of the greenhouse, camouflaging it with plastic flowers.

Wife Janet's quite happy with the arrangement, as she hasn't got three blokes in the lounge, drinking cans of beer and knocking them over on the carpet, and they can watch the football and scream and shout to their hearts' content, or simply put the world to rights over a couple of cans.

"The neighbours don't like it when we score a goal."

HOME IS WHERE THE SHED IS

Most men are content with simply having a shed or two at the bottom of the garden. Tony liked the idea of sheds so much, however, that he has extended them to his domestic arrangements. He lives in a barn, dividing his home between that and some of the smaller outlying sheds, which house everything from the toilet to the telephone. This structure allows him to break up the daily routine. "They're like a number of different nests, different worlds I can escape into."

In a former life, one of the sheds was a 40-foot-long single-decker bus, in which he took his children on holiday to Spain and on a tour of London. After it broke down in his yard, Tony decided he actually quite liked it there, added a trellis and began to use it as a kitchen. There's a practical reason for this, too – he hates the smell of cooking in the house: "It brings back memories of old Christmases with all my aunts and uncles, boiled cabbage and sprouts."

"We cooked bacon and eggs in it, outside Buckingham Palace."

THE NOTES OF A VISIONARY

Some years ago Ian presented a lecture on the importance of the shed in the world of buildings. "The shed has its own kind of aesthetic – one that has always been neglected in the teaching of architecture." He kept the lecture notes but lost them soon after, only to rediscover them years later… in his shed.

He's been adding to the foundation of those notes ever since, with newspaper cuttings, pictures and literary fragments. Some of these are pinned on the walls or piled on the floor of the shed, which is also home to a desk, a bed and a candelabrum. "It's a kind of dreaming place, where disparate things make something."

He's still fascinated with the way sheds present a Romantic opposition to uniformity and conformity, an opposition to Modernist edifices like skyscrapers. "Sheds are temporary structures, the kind of things people put up at crossroads, before villages and towns." And he loves the element of imperfection and contradiction, the fact that sheds are ramshackle, beautiful things.

"Sheds are outposts."

AUTHOR GORDON THORBURN'S SHEDS

Our 17th century farmhouse in Westmorland had eight acres, half a mile of trout stream and, as they say around there, sheds amain.

The one to make you jealous would be the 19th century sandstone haybarn. It was about 160 feet long and 40 feet wide, with a stone ramp up to the hayloft floor, below which were the original cattle byres.

In this our Great Shed we kept chickens, bred Golden Retrievers and stored the new village hall which was a second-hand Finnish wood prefab, to be erected as soon as... well, soon.

Incorporated in the Great Shed was the bull pen, where we kept pigs, fattened geese and succoured orphan lambs. Beside that was my tractor shed with garden tractor and trailer, early ride-on mower, antique rotavator, deadly brush cutter and all associated tools and rubbish. In the milking parlour (c.1950) we kept our furniture, moving it into the house as we worked through nine years of restoration.

Next to the house was a row of single-storey stone buildings looking like ancient cottages for Scottish peasants. The end one fell down. Next was the old smithy, where our friend Eric (qv) kept all his stuff, then The Cabin, where the farmer's wife used to cook for the men. Here I had DIY tools, timber, bags of cement, hand-wrought nails, circular saw and all sek mak o' tackle, and my fishing gear. Next came the log shed, the animal feed shed, and the old dairy where my wife kept her stock for her fruit and nut business and where lived Smartie and Muswold, the two cats charged with the protection of said stock.

We also had a proper hen hut in the front field, and Goose Hall. Now it's only a 1960s single garage and a three-roomed Victorian cellar...

**"A shedless man is a kiss
without a moustache."**

PHOTOGRAPHER JOHN BAXTER AND SHED

"Photography opens the door to meeting a lot of people and seeing a lot of things you wouldn't normally see" says John, a man who's seen more of Britain than most.

His CV includes work for clients as varied as *Crafts Magazine* and *Oasis Holiday Villages*, paintings and antiques catalogue photography, and collaborative projects with Gordon Thorburn on village cricket and the Appleby Rai. His favourite, however, is his profile of a champion leek grower from County Durham, who thanked him with a gift-box of enormous prize vegetables.

Between shoots, there are the pleasures of family life – wife of eight years, Johanne, and son Jack, who's two – and the stresses of supporting Blackburn Rovers. And, when he needs to get away from it all, he goes fell walking – well, unless it's raining, in which case there is always his shed.

There he can relax between the growing stack of radiators and the pile of paint rollers, and contemplate the coat of whitewash he's intending to give the walls in the very near future...

But, then, that might ruin the rugged ambience of the interior, and photographers are obsessed by these minutiae.

"Thorough, but not particularly organised."

PHOTOGRAPHER LAURA FORRESTER AND SHED

Just as Surrey, her county of birth and residence, combines cityscape and countryside, so Laura has covered a varied plot of photographic territory over the course of her short career.

Right from childhood days in her father Paul Forrester's studio, she always wanted to be a photographer. Her favourite project to date, "Bums", which she completed as part of her degree in Photography at Blackpool, is a large composite of prints, featuring the bottoms of twelve fellow students. Apparently, it tends to provoke a lot of interest.

So from backsides to back gardens: this is her first commercial project, which has taught her you can never judge a shed by its exterior... nor the blokes who own them.

Inspired by her visit into the inner sanctum of blokedom, she is already developing her own garden shed into something more than a junk repository. It's a modest but cosy affair, complete with net curtains at which most die-hard shed-men might wag a disapproving finger. But she insists she's not girlie. And she's not afraid of getting muddy.

"It's just another room of the house."

ACKNOWLEDGEMENTS

For help with research and assistance, thanks go to the following individuals and organisations:

Steve Ambrose; Johanne Baxter; John Baxter; Hannah Blake; Bernard Coote; Phil Davies; David Elton; Martin Dawes (The Star, Sheffield); Dave Elton; James Franklin (Project Films); Philip Goddard; Ruth Hamilton; Paul Harrington; Mike Holliday; Catherine Holmes; Derek Jones; Susan Jones; Philip Kolvin; Derek May; Alan Marshall; Adam Morris; Daniel Mountford; Sinead Murphy; Joanne O'Connell (Manchester Evening News); Annabel Other; Tony Paul; Geoff Porter (Lindisfarne Links); Arthur Reeder; Don Smith; Louisa Soper; James Starsmore; Simon Toft (The News, Portsmouth); Camilla Turner; Frank Westworth; Ken Whale; Brian Whitlie; Rosemary Wilkinson; Uncle Wilco.

Information on Lindisfarne, The Holy Island can be found at www.lindisfarne.org.uk.

All the shedmen featured can be contacted through the publishers.

PHOTOGRAPHIC CREDITS

John Baxter: pp 2, 6–10, 12–13, 18–23, 26–29, 32–33, 42–45, 50–51, 56–57, 60–63, 66–67, 72–73, 80–81, 84–87, 90–93, 100–101, 106–109, 116–119, 122–129, 132–133, 138–139, 142–143, 146–147, 150–153, 158–163, 168–173, 174, 177

Laura Forrester: pp 11, 14–17, 30–31, 34–41, 46–47, 52–55, 58–59, 64–65, 68–71, 74–79, 82–83, 88–89, 94–99, 102–105, 110–115, 120–121, 130–131, 134–137, 140–141, 144–145, 148–149, 154–157, 164–167, 175, 179, 183, 184

Alan Jefferis: pp 48–49

Pat Jones: pp 24–25

First published in 2006 by
New Holland Publishers (UK) Ltd
London • Cape Town • Sydney • Auckland
www.newhollandpublishers.com

Garfield House, 86–88 Edgware Road
London W2 2EA
United Kingdom

80 McKenzie Street
Cape Town 8001
South Africa

14 Aquatic Drive
Frenchs Forest, NSW 2086
Australia

218 Lake Road
Northcote, Auckland
New Zealand

182

10 9 8 7 6 5 4 3 2 1

ISBN 10: 1 84537 710 9
ISBN 13: 978 1 84537 710 6

Editors: Gareth Jones, Kate Parker
Editorial Direction: Rosemary Wilkinson
Designer: Paul Wright @ Cube
Photographers: John Baxter, Laura Forrester

Reproduction by Modern Age Repro House
Ltd, Hong Kong
Printed and bound by Craft Print International
Pte Ltd, Singapore

ALSO BY GORDON THORBURN:
*The Appleby Rai. Travelling people on a
thousand-year journey*. Photographs by
John Baxter.
Village Cricket, the genuine article.
Photographs by John Baxter.
43 Unsporting Moments. Illustrations by
Paul Davies.
The Buxton Baths Murders.